Tap it Tap.

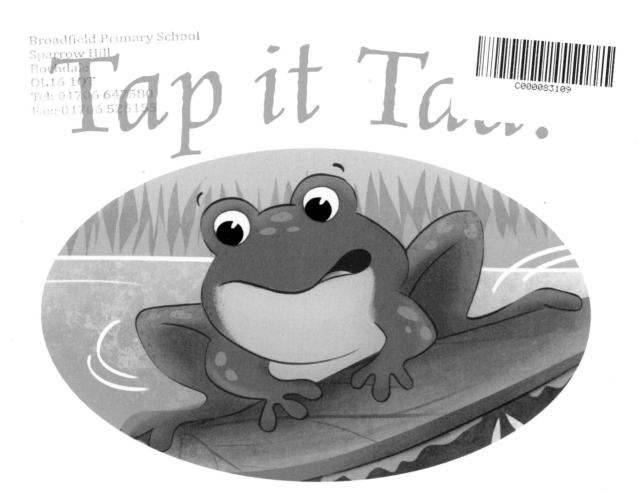

Written by Natasha Paul

Illustrated by Amy Zhing

Collins

Tap it Tad. Tap.

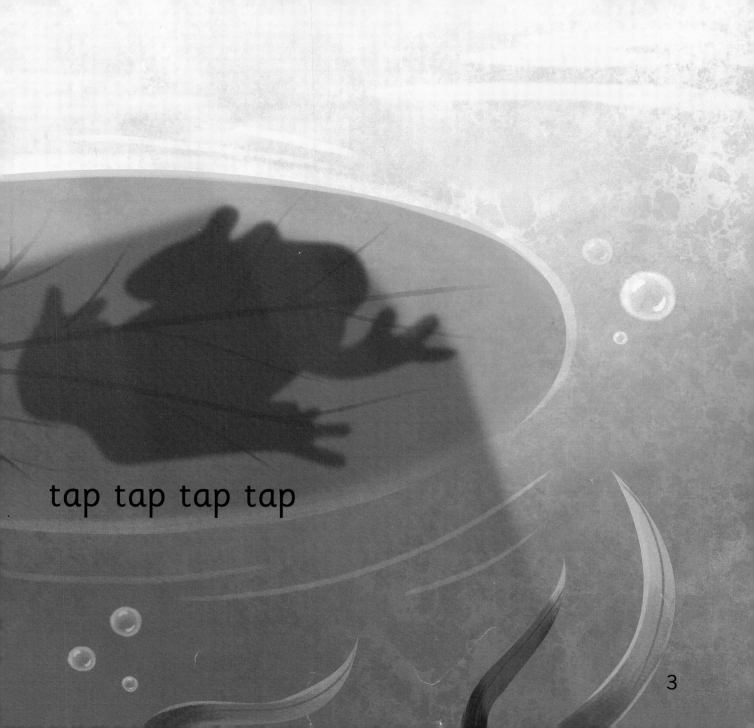

tap tap tap tap

3

Pat it Tad. Pat.

pit pat pit pat

Dad taps. Dad naps.

Pat a pad. Pat.

Dad sits. Dad tips.

Tip Dad in it!

Nip it. Nip it.

Nip at a pad.

It tips. It dips.

Mad Dad tips in!

14

🐾 Review: After reading 🐾

Use your assessment from hearing the children read to choose any GPCs, words or tricky words that need additional practice.

Read 1: Decoding

- Point to the word **Pat** on page 4. Ask the children sound out and then blend the word. (*P/a/t – **Pat***)
- Point to page 5 and ask them to find the word **pit** (emphasise the /i/ sound as you say the word).
- Repeat for pages 11 and 13. Point to **pad** and ask the children to sound out and blend. (*p/a/d – **pad***) Can they find and read **Dad** on page 13?
- Look at the "I spy sounds" pages (14–15). Point to the mole and say: I spy a /m/ in mole. Challenge the children to point to and name different things they can see containing a /m/ sound. Help them to identify /m/ items, asking them to repeat the word and listen out for the /m/ sound. (e.g. *moth, magnet, mud, chameleon, comet, worm, moon*)

Read 2: Prosody

- Model reading each page with expression to the children. After you have read each page, ask the children to have a go at reading with expression.

Read 3: Comprehension

- For every question ask the children how they know the answer. Ask:
  - On page 3, where is the frog? (e.g. *on top of the pond; on a lily pad*)
  - On pages 4 and 5, what is the tadpole trying to do? (e.g. *knock the frog off; get the frog to speak*)
  - What different things does the tadpole do to get Dad into the pond? (e.g. *pats him, tries to tip the pad over, nibbles the pad, pushes the pad again*)
  - How does Dad feel at the end of the story? Why? (e.g. *he is cross because the tadpole has woken him up and tipped him in the pond*)